Colours
around me

MB MACAW BOOKS

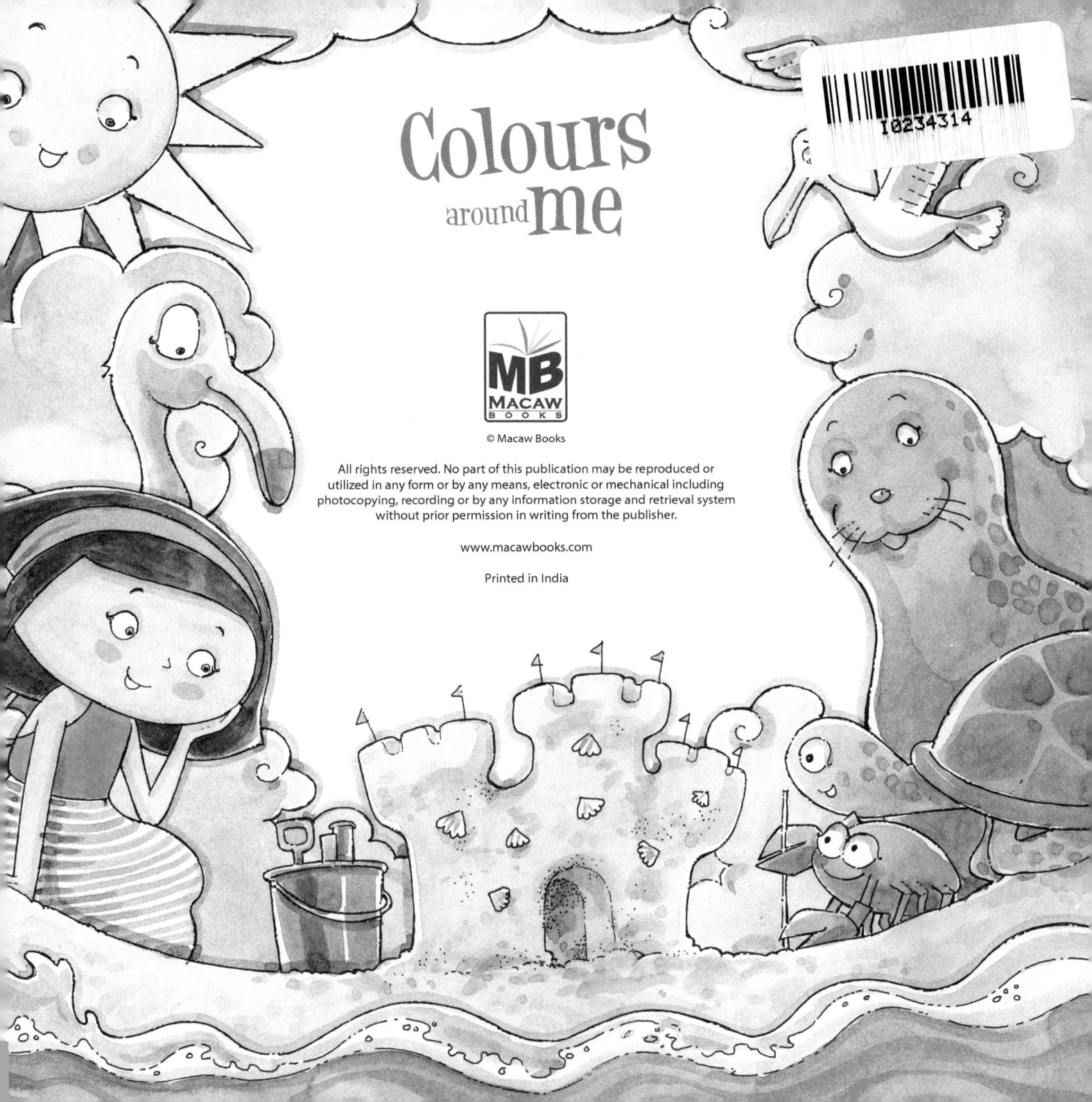

It was a bright day. Jenny was at the beach with her blue bucket and her silver shovel. She sat on the yellow sand by the blue sea.

She was building a grand golden sandcastle.

Jenny was very happy with her castle. But suddenly, a blue wave came her way. It was a great big wave, and it crashed upon her sandcastle. The sandcastle was washed away. Poor Jenny was very, very sad.

The white seagulls saw what had
happened. They opened their long
orange beaks and laughed, 'Ha! Ha! Ha!'

Jenny was angry. She shook her fist.

'I'll show you, you wait!' she shouted.

Jenny began to build a bigger sandcastle. She grabbed a friendly red crab. 'Will you guard my castle, brave mister crab?' she asked.

The yellow sun shone brightly
on Jenny and the red crab.

But again the large blue wave came down on Jenny's grand golden castle. 'Noo!' cried Jenny, as her castle fell into the sea.

'Ha! Ha! ha!' laughed the grey seals.
They clapped their grey hands with glee.

Now Jenny built an even bigger sandcastle. Her green turtle friend helped her make the towers tall. The red crab helped too.

But once again the blue wave
washed the castle away.

Jenny was very sad. She began to cry. 'Don't cry, dear Jenny,' said the red crab and the green turtle.

Then the pink flamingo said, 'Don't cry, dear Jenny. Make your castle farther from the sea.'

Then Jenny built her castle far from the sea. And this time, the blue wave could not reach it. It was the biggest sandcastle on the beach, with red flags and pink shells on it. Jenny was very happy. The white seagulls, the pink flamingo and the grey seals clapped happily.

At the
Pet Store

On Kimmy's tenth birthday,
Papa said, 'Darling, I think it is
time you had a pet of your own.'

Kimmy was so excited! Papa drove Kimmy to the pet store. Kimmy walked around the store to choose a pet.

'Hello! Hello!' said a parrot to Kimmy. She giggled in surprise. Then she walked on to see the other animals.

Next, she saw three furry little rabbits. 'Oh, how fluffy they are!' said Kimmy. She fed them some carrots and walked on.

'Woof Woof!' barked three little puppies. They wagged their tails at her. Kimmy played with them for some time and walked on.

Soon Kimmy saw a number of colourful snails. 'Ooh!' exclaimed Kimmy. The snails wriggled about slowly in their box.

Next, Kimmy reached the kitten cages. 'Puur! Purr!' said the kittens. How cute they were!

Cheep! Cheep!' squeaked a squirrel with a bushy tail. Kimmy opened its cage and the squirrel climbed up Kimmy's shoulder.

Kimmy walked on and reached an aquarium full
of colourful fish. A plump goldfish was swimming
inside a fish bowl. 'What a beautiful fish it is!' said
Kimmy.

Beside the aquarium
was a large monkey
cage. A brown
monkey climbed
the bars inside the
cage. Kimmy clapped
her hands in delight.

At another corner of the store was a hamster running in its cage. Kimmy spent a long time watching its wheel turn.

'Cheep! Cheep!' came the sound from another part of the store. 'Canaries!' squealed Kimmy. How beautiful the yellow canaries looked, as they flew about inside the cage.

Behind the canaries was a mouse cage. Kimmy gave it a piece of cheese to nibble on. 'I can't decide which pet to get!' said Kimmy.

'Well,' replied Papa, 'I think I know the perfect pet for you.' He led Kimmy to a beautiful golden pony. Kimmy hugged the pony out of happiness.

'I shall name her Sugar and ride her everywhere,' said Kimmy.

How happy she was to finally have a pet!

www.ingramcontent.com/pod-product-compliance
Lightning Source LLC
LaVergne TN
LVHW082324080426
835508LV00042B/1528

9 781640 358133